Web Fluent

The Faster, Easier Way to Build Your Web Business

Being *Web Fluent* means you're fluent in the art of Web business and you understand how to create something genuine—as well as earn money with it.

By

Nelson Bates

BestWebsite® LLC   Published 2012   United States of America
Ver. 1.0   All rights reserved   Copyright©.

The Best Website book is protected under United States and International copyright laws, among others being 17 U.S.C. Sec 102(a).

No portion of this book may be reproduced or distributed without the expressed written consent of the owner. Should this copyright law be violated, BestWebsite, LLC must prosecute to the full extent of the law.

If you purchased this book from someone other than BestWebsite, LLC, Amazon, Barnes & Noble or affiliates it is an unlawful copy and the Author did not receive credit for the purchase. Please email best@bestwebsite.com or call 407-963-7331 to report.

Additionally, any electronic retrieval and recovery system used to store and disseminate this text and or images is strictly prohibited.

ISBN-13: 978-1468115932
ISBN-10: 1468115936

Bates, Nelson – Author, Entrepreneur, Web Marketer

Library of Congress
Copyright Office
101 Independence Avenue, S.E.
Washington, DC 20559-6000

1 2 3 4 5 6 7 8 9 10

Web Fluent: The Faster, Easier Way to Build Your Web Business

To my Dad..

I'm awestruck by your dedication to our Family.

Thank you for providing an unwavering foundation for me to grow and learn.

you.. inspire.. me..

I love you!

Web Fluent: The Faster, Easier Way to Build Your Web Business

Intro:

This book is meant to be a lightning fast read. The goal is to get you building a successful Web business or improving an existing one as fast as possible.

It's for entrepreneurs and aspiring entrepreneurs. It's about building a successful Web company with your unique compelling passion; it's about starting something brilliant; it's about sharing it with others and creating a valuable asset you own along the way.

The book stems from my sixteen years in the business; I've built a string of successful, highly profitable Web businesses.

I provide a unique perspective because it's I who does the web design, graphic design, database coding, comes up with the products, develops the marketing campaigns and makes adjustments along the way—in the process of building a Web business that has lasting impact and creates wealth.

It's important that you're hearing these techniques first-hand. Don't worry, you don't need all these skills yourself; as a matter of fact, you'll probably only need one or two. I can show you the best ways to accomplish everything you need to start and build your own Web business that makes money.

Let's get to work!

Web Fluent: The Faster, Easier Way to Build Your Web Business

Contents:

I. First-up.. The Essential 9 things you should do to make your Web business a success.
II. Then... fifteen of my best, most inspiring and informative articles to get you prepped and ready to build your Web business.
III. Next... on to the specifics with tips and tools for web design, blog platform, Facebook and other social media marketing.
IV. Then... on to a case study with **Jim Weber**, formally with ESPN, who has built an incredible college sports website with amazing traffic and a great revenue model.
V. And finally... a closing chapter to ensure you're off on the right foot to starting and building your own brilliantly successful Web business.

Family Bonus!
A chapter by **Lana Bates**, that's right, my

Mom! She's the smartest marketer I know. It was Mom who told me in 1995 **"this Web thing is going to be big!"** ...I said OK, OK, I'll check out after my second nap. But you know what? "The Web thing" has been my entire career thus far.

Mom has always been leading the curve and she'll be talking about where this whole **"web thing"** is going in the future...an insightful, important read.

And last but not least, *WordPress* expert and brother, **Sterling Bates**, gives a complete rundown of exactly how to get your *WordPress* website up and running in a flash.

But make no mistake...Mom and Sterling are not included in this book because they are family. They are included because they are the best-of-the-best and I credit much of my success to them. Now it's their turn to help you!

Web Fluent: The Faster, Easier
Way to Build Your Web Business

What is Web Fluent?

Being fluent in Web business means you understand some fundamental truths about how to create something genuine—as well as earn money with it.

If you're *Web Fluent*, you know that 50 connected Facebook Fans are more powerful than 5,000 casual Fans or even 50,000 casual Twitter followers.

You know to focus your efforts on <u>one</u> important goal that you have compelling passion for and happily ignore the rest.

You know that starting something brilliant doesn't mean you need a brilliant idea...you just need a good idea to start and then you can turn it into something brilliant along the way.

You know that spending more than an hour researching keywords for your brand is a waste of time. You know it's better to do one amazing blog post a month than ten good ones.

If you're Web Fluent, you know that blogging is one of your best friends, both for connecting with others and focusing your thoughts. You know that if you're an entrepreneur you need to learn the blogging platform yourself or a web design program to start your business, because if you try to hire it out, you'll drain your bank account before your business has a chance to succeed.

You also know it's better to connect with the people you already have rather than to try and build a bigger list. You know that having 1,000 True Fans is plenty enough to create a rich life in all its meanings.

You know that by the time you start your idea, until the time it starts to achieve the success you dreamed of, will likely be two years. You know that on some projects you will need to be bold...or you'll be boring.

You also know the exhilarating feeling of satisfaction that comes with providing something genuine to others and making money along the way...and that it's OK to make a lot of money.

Are you Web Fluent?

If not, let's get you there as fast as possible.

The Essential 9 Most Important Things.

This list originally started in my *Best Website* book in 2008. It proved to be so popular I've updated it for this book.

It lists the 9 most-important things you can do as an Entrepreneur to make your Web business successful.

1. **If you're considering ten different business ideas..** try one business idea—marketed ten different ways.

   Put all your eggs in one basket, it's scary, but it's what successful Entrepreneurs do to make sure something works.

   It's much easier to get one idea to work, rather than ten. Trying too many is almost guaranteeing none will work.

Which idea to choose?

Choose the one that excites you the most to tell someone else about.

2. Learn enough WordPress®, TypePad®, DreamWeaver®, Expression Web® etc., to update your own website.

It takes hours of reading and fumbling around to gain control, but once you have it, it will undoubtedly be one of your most powerful assets as an Entrepreneur.

*WordPress how-to Chapter included later in the book

3. Before you switch your computer on.. have the <u>one</u> most important task you need to accomplish that day in mind—and then do it before anything else.

The results are stunning, ..no-kidding.

4. Write three remarkable articles.. that relate to your product and that highlight your passion and knowledge.

This is difficult I know, but if done well can pay amazing dividends for years to come.

5. **Setup a free Squidoo.com page..** and post your articles.

   This is an excellent way to gain valuable prospects from the vibrant *Squidoo* business community (currently a top 100 Website).

   As a bonus, it boosts your Search Engine rankings by targeting the right laser targeted keywords.

6. **Select three laser targeted keywords..** to target in your Articles —on your Website or Blog.

   Using laser targeted keywords means a much faster time gaining rankings and traffic (less than a month), and a much higher conversion rate into sales. Use *Google Suggest* to help you select them.

Example: The keyword "internet marketing book" took me 11 days to gain a first page Google ranking; it drives almost 50 Unique Visitors a day to BestWebsite.com and averages 4 sales.

7. Press Release with PRWeb.com..

This is a fantastic way to use your three laser targeted keywords in a Press Release posted on their top-ranked website and link back to yours.

Not only do they boost your search rankings but they also announce your business and product to the right media and guarantee coverage or they'll run your release again.

8. Add the free Google Analytics code to your Website or Blog..

It's not only the best web traffic reporting software available. It lets you see who's coming to your site, how they got there, and which keywords you're receiving traffic from.

But more importantly, it gives Google valuable information about how people use your site and what they use it for—allowing them to rank your site higher and for better keywords because they understand what your business is about.

9. **Remember the Entrepreneur Motto to..** Start Something Brilliant, —Be Bold or You're Boring, and to — Create Something Genuine.

    How to implement this Motto is described through-out the book with examples.

Compelling Passion!

Forget blogging, a FaceBook page, Twitter, linking strategies, search engine optimization, etc....if you're not creating your products, services or marketing campaigns with truthful compelling passion, your end result will likely be a flat response at best, or more likely a complete flop.

When you find your passion and apply it to what you're working on people recognize it immediately; they gravitate toward it, they share it with others; they help you spread the word effortlessly.

I hope you're creating something brilliant with your compelling passion—we need it. Passion, especially compelling passion, is about the only thing in short supply.

Be Bold or Be Boring.

About every week ...at some point, I need this advice.

Let's go! Pick it up! Find some courage.

Time to make the business call I'm scared to make. Time to send the e-mail I'm worried about. Time to pitch the idea I might get ridiculed for.

It's time to risk doing something scary, to do something great. NOW ...not later.

Exercising the "getting scary things done" muscle makes it easier to do whatever you're scared of again and again. The risks become less and the rewards become greater.

Be Bold or Be Boring!

Good luck, I know it's difficult. But it's worth it.

My Simple Social Media Marketing Strategy.

I've heard social media marketing described as "a thousand baseballs falling from the sky, which ones do I grab?" I'm in the business every day and even I get confused at times. I thought I'd describe what has worked for me in hopes it will illuminate a clear path for you.

With social media it's not big numbers that count, it's the number of people who trust you. Sometimes people forget that...including me.

I've chosen one medium—blogging—to use to create value and trust. I have it automatically posted to my Facebook, Twitter and sent to my email list. That means as soon as I write an article and click post in my Blog account, it posts to my Blog page, business Facebook page, Twitter account *and* emails my entire list automatically.

It has been incredibly helpful to focus on one medium and not become scattered in thought. I know I'd like a dedicated Facebook and Twitter presence, however, not at the expense of detracting from my original focus, my blog. About a year ago I stopped looking to make my e-mail list bigger (it's currently about 1,700 subscribers). Instead I put my effort into connecting with the people already here.

Here are the specifics of this strategy. I set up my blog through TypePad.com. Then I set up a Facebook Fan Page and used the free utility RSS Graffiti (you add this once your Fan page is set up) to grab the posts from my blog account and post them on my Facebook page. Then I selected the box inside my TypePad account to post my blog directly to my Twitter account by entering my Twitter account username and password. Finally I signed up for Feedblitz to grab my new blog posts and put them in an email to my subscriber list.

If you try to manage these accounts individually instead of automatically you'll probably go bonkers.

Also, if you're under the impression you will read enough to eventually become comfortable starting a Blog, Facebook page or Twitter account, you probably won't.

Web Fluent: The Faster, Easier Way to Build Your Web Business

You'll be completely uncomfortable, it will feel wrong, you'll be confused during set-up, your initial layout won't be what you want and you'll feel like you're not sure what to say anyway.

It's best to just get moving. Kids are good at this. They just start clicking things. And yes they break them, but the sooner you break them the sooner you can fix them and start sharing your compelling passion with others and creating a valuable asset you own.

Create something genuine and others will do your social media marketing for you by sharing it. It's that simple.

One Way to Create a Powerful Impact With Your Business.

I wanted to share the story of when things changed for me and how it enhanced my business. It involves the synergy of some great portrait photos, brilliant business cards and a professional website that when combined created a fantastically powerful impact.

I used terrible business cards for ten years. I'm sure you've seen them, the ones you print at home and everyone knows it. Cheap, thin cards with no pizzazz, just an ordinary, bland card. About six months ago I found a print company called Moo.com. They specialize in printing business cards that leave an impression.

Not only are the cards bigger and thicker than most anything out there, they feel silky to the touch. As soon as someone receives one from you, they know you are someone of-note, someone different.

Also, during the last two years I've been getting reasonably good at photography and was able to get some great,
professional self-portraits to use in

Web Fluent: The Faster, Easier Way to Build Your Web Business

business. I uploaded the photos to *Moo* and put three different photos on the backs of my cards.

Now...having spent so many years with bad business cards, the change in handing out one of these thick, professional cards was positively dramatic.

Not only did people start to act more engaged as soon as they touched it, but sometimes even before I got back to the office I would see they had already been online, signed up for my blog and sent me a thank-you e-mail about meeting me.

But there's one more piece to this puzzle. I had the same photos on my website as well and one big one on my home page. Something about a nice, large, clear photo of you makes people feel they know you better.

It created the perfect complement of seeing me in person, having my business card as a visual reminder and then seeing me again on my site along with my full bio. This synergy has a powerful impact on people and I believe signifies you've reached a different level in business.

The best thing is, it's under your control whether you achieve the synergy or not.

No one to ask, no marketplace to figure out; just your decision to do it.

Stop Talking and Start Walking.

It didn't take me long to realize I'm not smarter than anyone else. I'm pretty average in fact. What I have noticed about myself however, is that as soon as I have an idea I believe is a good one, I stop talking about it and start moving forward.

Often I'll start with only limited knowledge of the market and only a reasonable sense of where I'd like to end up. I often find myself alone, cold on some rainy treacherous path that usually feels hopeless most of the way. But I always seem to end up at the finish line. I complete what I start one way or the other. What feels like the wrong path for most of the journey I know is the right path to eventual success.

I hear great ideas from people all the time. But most people are talkers not doers. It's probably best to get moving right now, start learning in the marketplace instead of guessing what you think will happen or gathering more information. You probably have enough or even more than enough information already.

What's the one project you believe in and aren't doing right now? It doesn't matter if you have all the data. I'd rather see you get lost along the way than find you back at the starting line (aka the failure line if you never start walking). It's easy to stay at the starting line, most of our friends hang-out there.

So stop talking and start walking...please.

The Puzzle Pieces Will Fit.

If you've been trying to get a business started or your existing one is struggling, please take comfort in knowing that almost everyone is trying to fit their puzzle pieces together as well.

It's a much tougher business environment to get deals done, products launched, businesses humming again. It's OK to be frustrated, it's part of the game and ironically part of the satisfaction comes from figuring it out. When you do, you smile. It's fun, it was worth it.

Maybe you'll use pieces from different puzzles and yours will look a little funny when it's put together. As long as you get them to work, it doesn't matter.

Keep going. Work for the long term. A confused business environment is the best time of all to start something brilliant!

Actioners Make All the Money.

Strategizer vs. Actioner

One of the most important factors in business is this: The people who make the most money, run the most successful websites, write the best books and blogs, are the Actioners.

Actioners are the people who start a business with only limited knowledge of the market. They know that by the time they have an idea they believe can work, it's already time to start acting on the idea.

Actioners know that additional knowledge will probably hurt them; they know reading another book, going to another seminar or having another strategy session to look at the "data" will only serve to confuse them.

Actioners know that it's important to get their product/service/website launched now so they can start testing different marketing ideas and making and learning from mistakes.

They know that the Strategizers will be busy planning and theorizing about the marketplace, while the Actioner is learning truths about the market and how to win it.

I'm not advocating jumping in haphazardly or before you're ready. I'm advocating that you need to recognize that by the time you have an idea you believe can work, it's time to start being an Actioner!

Good News for Women in Web Business.

Ladies, if you've found building a Web business difficult it's not exactly your fault. Virtually every aspect of the computer was designed through the eyes of a geeky male computer nerd. Think of a young Bill Gates in a garage throwing a party where the main source of fun is program coding.

Whether it's the operating system, web design, graphic design, programming or Domain Name Servers, its logic was set up through a male brain.

Web Fluent: The Faster, Easier Way to Build Your Web Business

On average, your start-up will likely be a bit tougher than your male counterparts. However, if you can push past the initial technical stage, your communication and organization skills now put YOU in the advantage.

The hill looks ugly on the climb up, but it's pretty on the other side ... I promise.

p.s. Literally some of the best graphic designers and programmers I've ever met were women. I'm not saying women aren't as smart as men, I'm only saying some of the start-up issues come more intuitively, in general, to men.

Go For the Money First, Passion Second.

I'm sure you've heard to choose something you're passionate about as a business and your passion for it will eventually break down all barriers on your way to success.

Unfortunately, too often that isn't the case.

I suggest a small change to the approach... I agree with the first part—to choose something you're passionate about. But here's a departure from the second part of that equation.

Find where the money is to be made when you're starting out because if you don't solve the money issue soon(meaning the business is reasonably profitable), you'll have to go back to doing whatever you were doing before that you didn't like and had absolutely zero passion for.

Once the money issue is solved, slowly but surely morph your business into what you're most passionate about.

That's how you get to do what you love AND make BIG money doing it.

The Bottleneck.

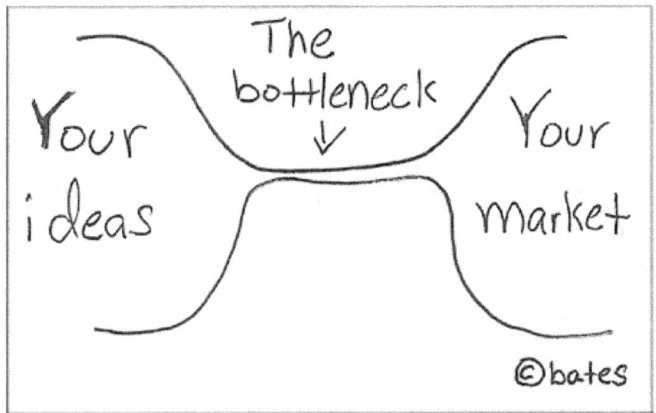

The bottleneck is anything that blocks your ideas from becoming a reality in the marketplace.

Everyone has bottlenecks, some people's are completely closed. Most people's bottlenecks are barely open and incredibly difficult to get anything through…including my own at times.

Interestingly, most successful people operate with a barely open bottleneck.

They have learned the bottleneck will never be easy to get things through. They decided not to wait around until it got easier, it won't. Instead they just practice getting things through and solving the few things that must be solved to keep it open; they constantly put out things like blog posts, videos, campaigns and products into the marketplace.

Maybe you're lacking some technical skills, money to start, you're going through a divorce, illness, your kid is in jail, you're in jail...whatever.

The key is to identify the one or two things that are truly blocking you and focus on them until they open the bottleneck—at least wide-enough to get some things through.

Example, I have difficulty typing. It hurts my hands and the radiation from my computer monitor bothers me enough to make me slightly sick. This is a bit ridiculous because I've run a Web business the last sixteen years and write and build Web companies and websites as a career.

So, to fix this bottleneck that blocked my access to my market. I got the software where you speak into a microphone and it turns your speech into text (*Dragon*

Web Fluent: The Faster, Easier Way to Build Your Web Business

Naturally Speaking) and then got a low-radiation monitor with a 3M radiation screen blocker.

My question is, what's your bottleneck? What problem needs to be solved to reach your marketplace. Cut out other people as often as you can; how can YOU get to your market the fastest. The sooner you're there, the sooner you can start getting true knowledge about your business environment and stop guessing about it.

For intermediate and advanced Web entrepreneurs, the bottleneck is probably you. You're trying to make a hard decision of whether or not to do something. My advice, do the one that scares you the most. Even if you fail, the knowledge you gain will brilliantly outweigh the cost.

For those who haven't broken into their market yet, one of the best ways to do it is to start a blog—just start typing, posting, putting things out there into the Web. Keep doing it and at least some of your market will eventually find you.

Ironically, the bottleneck is a good thing. It's a barrier to entry. Most people never figure theirs out. That's good for you because it keeps your competition out.

Web Fluent: The Faster, Easier
Way to Build Your Web Business

Where's Your Money?

Don't spend too much time on the left-hand side. Your business, your assets, your money is on the right-hand side.

Researching		Blog Post
Planning		Website Launch
Meetings		Signed Agreement
Brainstorming		Interview Given
Building		Product Launch
Testing		Book Release
Writing		Press Release

Getting Past *The Corner* is What Makes You Wealthy.

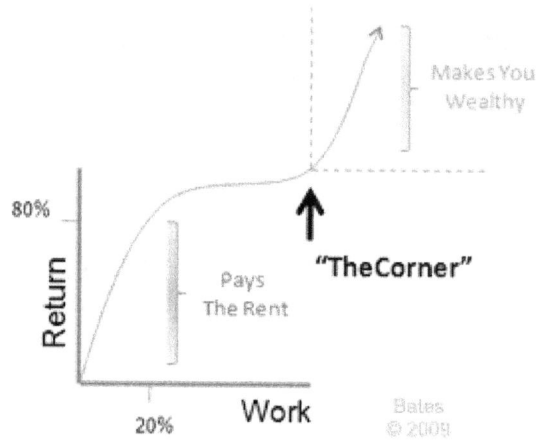

Yes it's true, 20% of the work earns 80% of the results. The reason to sometimes complete the 80% of work that only earns 20% of the results, is because of *The Corner.*

When you complete the work that others will not, by the end of it you'll be on a **new** graph that begins where the old one left off, and the additional benefits can be extraordinary.

Example: If the additional work you do allows you to become #1 in your niche market, that can mean the 80% of work

Web Fluent: The Faster, Easier Way to Build Your Web Business

returns 1,000% or more instead of only 20%.

Why? Because by completing the work others won't gives you access to a whole new market previously invisible to you.

To me the answer is ... do the work that gets you past *The Corner*. It's always worth it!

Notes: Every one of the web businesses I founded has followed this graph. It has been amazingly consistent.

Also, it's not to say you do this with every product or business you have. However, if you BELIEVE it can make it past *The Corner*...Go for it! You're probably right!

Part 2

Specific Web Design Advice and Results on Web Marketing Campaigns I've Run

Making Web Design Easier.

First up, shouldn't web design be easier by now? They've had at least 17 years to work on it.

Unfortunately no, it's even more difficult and complicated now and part of the reason is the sheer number of choices of tools you can use to build your website (most people routinely use the wrong one).

But, with a few important pieces of information, you'll be able to start with the right tool and get moving fast.

So first let's consider your situation and what you're trying to accomplish. Then I'll be able to recommend the right tool.

The first situation is where an internet business is your main goal, your primary means of earning your income, or at least you'd like it to be. The second situation is if you're a traditional brick-and-mortar business that is looking to gain clients/referrals/prospects from your website.

There are also two categories for full time Web business owners. This depends on if you have a lot of products or just a few

Web Fluent: The Faster, Easier Way to Build Your Web Business

products to sell. If you have a lot of products go with WordPress to build your site. They have plenty of prebuilt add-ons for database and shopping cart checkout. *(See step-by-step WordPress chapter later.)*

If you only have a few products or services and you've got time to learn it or pay a designer for custom design, then go with the most powerful, no restrictions on design, Macromedia Dreamweaver or my personal favorite Microsoft Expression Web, both around $199.

There are steep learning curves for both, but these are the grand-daddy's of them all and if you'll be doing serious Web business, then these are your best choices. *(See the Best Website book—my first book—for detailed step-by-step Microsoft Expression Web help.)*

It's certainly not to say you can't run a big time website using WordPress, but you'll always be confined by what their templates and add-ons can do. They are however, getting much better and have amazing flexibility at this point.

But don't think it will be easy if you start adding a bunch of add-ons like a database of products, shopping cart, discussion forums, etc. Also, your website will still always kind of look like a bunch of other websites.

However, since many Web designers specialize in *WordPress*, you can get most good websites done for $1,500 to start and it goes up from there with maintenance and/or modifications. *WordPress* will probably be the choice for most people.

My recommendation if you'll be doing it yourself and you'd just like a reasonably basic site, is to use *TypePad*.

It's what I use for my blog and it has the ability to create stand alone pages with info, videos, graphics, payment button, pretty much anything you want to put on a webpage in addition to the regular blog post page. The blogging platform has been moving steadily into full- fledged web design programs, but with restrictions.

A *TypePad* blog, with your own URL is what I also recommend if you're a brick-and-mortar business looking to drive customers to you.

Web Fluent: The Faster, Easier Way to Build Your Web Business

Also, let me make this recommendation after watching people try and build their Web businesses over the last 16 years. As much as you want to pay someone else to take care of the details and build the site for you, don't. It's likely they won't build what you want and they will charge you more than want to pay. At some point you'll find yourself whimpering in a dark corner wondering what happened to your life.

It's much easier to save the money and grab the power. Go to *TypePad*, sign up for a basic account and spend one-hour reading the instructions. You will now be ahead of 99.8% of everyone else on the planet.

You can have your first post up on the world wide web within hours, with all the social media buttons, comments section, and search engine optimized links automatically posted on the page.

By doing it this way you are staying in control, you're grabbing the power for yourself. It will mean less time in the short and long term and less money (to pay someone else and more money for you) because it's you who understands how the blog platform works and how to use it best for your situation.

Now, a bit of bad news...at some point during designing your site you'll find yourself back in that corner curled up in the fetal position whimpering. I know, I know, I'm sorry. This is because you'll want the software to do something you need and you can't figure out how to do it. This is OK and normal; all designers end up there at some point. Just post an eLance job for $25 for someone to show you how to do it.

Definition:: eLance is an online marketplace where you can post large or small projects and have qualified freelancers from around the World post how they can help you do what you need done and for what price.

This is a very effective way to do things and is how you become more and more powerful. You're like a wizard learning new spells that work on the Web. The more you know and practice, the better.

Forgive me if you are still confused. This is actually part of the advantage as well. It keeps your competition out of the game. By selecting the right tool and learning it, you'll be well on your way to building your successful Web company!

Web Fluent: The Faster, Easier Way to Build Your Web Business

Warning.

There is R-rated content on the next page, if you're sitting next to someone, please take caution.

(Intentionally left blank.)

The Provocateur Project.

OK, so how in the world did this happen?

Well, —long story short. After years of creating marketing campaigns that were predicable, I decided to follow my own mantra to be Bold and not Boring.

I did the photography, post-production and launched the campaign not knowing if I'd be run out of town.

Please read the "Unexpected Wisdom Gained from the Provocateur Project" later in the book to see the results.

But first, here's the text from the campaign...

The mission for this campaign is to **ignite your inspiration** to find a different, more compelling way to run your business, launch a product or create a campaign.

It doesn't need to be provocative, just not boring and forgettable. Something **DARING!** Something that takes courage to put out under public scrutiny.

It's not about playing it safe or following the rules. It's about finding the guts to **Be Bold or Be Boring** and create something fascinating...captivating...enchanting.

No one in the Web marketing industry does anything like this. I've mixed what is traditionally a high-fashion type of provocative marketing campaign with one of my mantras to **Start Something Brilliant**.

It took 3-months to get this shot and another 3-months to be brave enough to release it. Please forgive me if I've offended you, it's not my intention. It was to try something new, something that scares me, inspires me and hopefully a few others as well.

And the best news of all, it's all for a good cause, 100% of the proceeds from Prints are donated to the National Breast Cancer Foundation, Inc.

Notes: To see the full campaign as it was intended with music and animation, please see BestWebsite.com

I did the Photography, image Post-Production, Flash Design and Web Design. Best viewed on a computer with Flash installed.

The Provocateur Project
Part 2.

An idea to earn a lot more money.

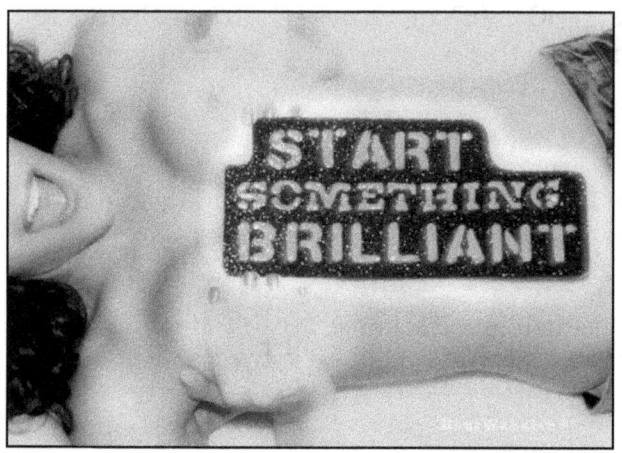

Many entrepreneurs are getting killed on price because they offer only one service and have to compete with workers around the globe that will do that same job a lot cheaper.

When you group services together and sell them as a package, you can make a lot more than if you sold them individually.

Unless you're in the top 1% of web designers, programmers, photographers, architects, engineers or really any profession that sells a single service, you have likely been priced down to the bone by your competition.

To illustrate: When I put together this upcoming *"Start Something Brilliant Campaign"* for BestWebsite.com, I did the photography, then graphic design in Photoshop, then imported the images into the Flash movie, then mocked the campaign up online with web design and finally created a promotional campaign to release it.

This campaign would have likely paid me around $1,500 if I was trying to sell the services individually to a client. However, If I pitch it to a potential client that I do everything including launch it as a campaign, this same campaign pays a minimum of $15,000 (to as high as $150,000) depending on how much involvement the client wants from me in rolling out the marketing campaign.

Service	separately	if sold grouped
Photography	$400	$4,000+
Photoshop	$300	$3,000+
Flash	$200	$2,000+
Web Design	$200	$2,000+
Internet Marketing	$400	$4,000+
	$1,500+	$15,000+

Is it difficult to learn all these skills? It definitely is. But if you're trying to offer your clients only one of these services, you are likely at near poverty right now ... I know, I've done it.

You might think you should offer a discount when you group services, and in some cases this is true. However, if you add the magic ingredient that means you'll be participating in developing the creative elements for the campaign and *that* means you'll be helping with the marketing strategy. This ties it together and lets you earn a lot more money from selling the same services.

Web Fluent: The Faster, Easier Way to Build Your Web Business

The interesting part is you're likely doing it already. You're probably brainstorming and coming up with ideas for the client anyway.

Why not present yourself as the guru you probably already are and bundle a number of services together to make a lot more money.

It's incredible how many people sell themselves short on what they know, including me sometimes. I remember when I was about halfway through writing my first Web business book, I wondered to myself... "Why in the world do I think I know what I'm talking about?"

I still didn't believe in myself even though I had more than 12 years' experience building web businesses.

Then I thought, "if not me then who?" So I understand if you're hesitant at first, but find the courage to present yourself as the expert or spend the time to become one if you're not yet. Part of being an expert is taking the difficult step to present yourself as one.

In some ways it might seem unreasonable to have to be a professional in multiple services, however the marketplace doesn't care; However, if you know that, you can prosper and thrive.

Maybe you don't have to bundle as many services as I have, but for each service you can bundle with another service, you can synergistically boost your income. Grouping at least three services is where you'll start to see the true power of the Law of Synergy.

Notes: Why do a provocative campaign?

I've been fascinated by the successful marketing campaigns by Tom Ford's fashion brand and wanted to create something similar. No one in my industry does anything like this. It's me following my own advice of "Being Bold or Being Boring."

Anatomy of a Marketing Campaign.

This was a much tougher photo-shoot and campaign to put together than I originally anticipated. It seems like a simple shoot, however it took me months of prep-work to find the right model who was not only professional and a delight-to-work-with, but amazingly photogenic as well.

The "**Start Something Brilliant**" signs were made with 3-Dimensional Ink that is normally applied to T-Shirts and I found this great reflective black and white paper to put it on using stencils.

It took the full hour of shooting to get the exact right positioning of the signs and angle, as well as the lighting.

-> **Photographer:** Nelson Bates

-> Shot with a **Canon 400D** using a **50mm Canon Portraiture-lens**

-> Lighting using a **430EX Speedlight** with **Gary Fong** light diffuser attached.

-> Post-production of images in **Photoshop.**

-> Flash production using **Amara Slide-Show builder.**

-> Web Design using **Microsoft Expression Web.**

Unexpected Wisdom Gained From 'The Provocateur Project'.

Launching this type of provocative campaign allowed me to travel a business path I had not experienced before.

Since the campaign is R-rated, I wanted to wait until the evening to post it so most of the people would see it at night and hopefully not while at work.

So I'm in my home office waiting around until 9 p.m. EST to press send. It's taken me six months to complete the campaign and I've written and rewritten and reworked the campaign and article that goes with it many times over.

I've also received a ton of advice and counsel before releasing it. A fair amount of it was negative, but certainly some of it positive as well.

At the exact moment I clicked the Post button to send the campaign to my 1,800 blog email readers, FaceBook Fans, Twitter followers—many of whom I've spent years building trust with—and brought the campaign live on my main website, I realized I've now stepped out in front of everyone and called attention to what I've done. I'm putting myself out-there and vulnerable to public scrutiny, possible anger and backlash.

I was standing in a place where I could be praised and celebrated, but also the same place where I can get hit with tomatoes and possibly rocks.

I was very nervous and wondering if I'd just done the dumbest thing in my business career.

So what happened?..

One week after the campaign came out, according to Google Analytics more than 531 Unique Visitors have viewed the first page of the campaign, staying on that page more than 3 minutes and 11 seconds.

Of those 531 people, 119 of them clicked through to see the second image and of those 119 people 53 of those clicked through to the Behind-the-Scenes page.

And of the 53 who made it to the end, not one of them left the site on that page. Meaning they stuck around to see other things on my site.

I only had a few people who were truly angry and offended and that posted comments on the campaign page. I'm glad that there were people who came to my defense.

I didn't face a wave of unsubscribes from my email list as I had feared. I actually had less than normal. Everyone's list loses some subscribers 8on each mailing due to ISP removal, people moving on or dead email accounts.

I'm both appalled and inspired by what I've done. I'm appalled, because it's such a blatant play-to-sex. I'm inspired because of what I've learned along the journey of attempting to be creative in my approach and finding enough guts to finally release it; and the wisdom gained from doing something that completely scared me.

I encourage you to find one thing that truly scares you. Something daring that allows you to step out in front of everyone, at the least for a moment, and call for people to notice what you've done and face the praise or backlash or more likely, both.

Web Fluent: The Faster, Easier Way to Build Your Web Business

Using WordPress® to Build and Manage Your Website.

By **Sterling Bates** WordPress® Expert User.

For this article I am going to talk about using some of the recent advances and technology that increase your options to quickly and easily build successful websites.

One of the simplest and quickest ways to have a professional looking website that is both modern and easy is to use WordPress.

Most people know WordPress as one of the top three blogging application/platforms. But in reality it is a powerful Content Management System. As of

January 18, 2011 WordPress was used by 13% of the top million biggest websites. The high usage of WordPress and open source nature mean good things for entrepreneurs and recent advances have opened up new options. Specifically you can use WordPress as the backbone of your website.

Why use WordPress?
- Free and heavily tested (a big advantage of open source)

- Easy to host and setup (basic PHP and MySQL database and automatically supported by most hosts with a basic/economy plan)

- Easy to get the look you want (there are thousands of free themes and the premium themes [for pay] can be stunningly professional for less than $100.)

- Easy to maintain (especially for non-programmers)

- Easy to update your content (often a problem with a normal website if you are not a developer)

- Easy to expand and add professional capability (there are thousands of prebuilt, heavily tested plugins to expand the WordPress functionality for almost any imaginable use)

- Readily recognized and understood by most developers and bloggers (making it easy to find someone to help you)

Most non-programmers, regular entrepreneurs, using some of the choices I will mention can get a

Web Fluent: The Faster, Easier Way to Build Your Web Business

professional website up and running themselves for less than $100 and in about 3 hours. This often includes many advanced features you would normally pay a
developer $2,000 or more to implement for you. Is that enough of a reason to keep reading?

In the tradition of the Nelson's style we will be going into specific details and simple steps so you can do this yourself.

Here are the topics I will cover:
1. Picking a Theme
2. Hosting
3. Basic Setup
4. Basic Content
5. Plugins and Widgets
6. Advanced Setup
7. Advanced Content
8. Other Alternatives to WordPress
9. Conclusion

NOTE: I am receiving no benefit or compensation from any of the products I may list. This is simply a record of the products I have tried and liked.

1. Picking a Theme

First thing I would do before doing anything else is make sure you can find a WordPress theme that fits your business. If you can't, the only you thing you lost was a little time looking at themes and you can look for another approach. There are a lot of free WordPress themes. If you get one that fits your business and does what you want you are lucky. I use premium themes (typically less than $100). More specifically, I use
premium themes that provide many configuration options to provide me with the most flexibility so I can get exactly what I want out of the website.

My favorites to date have come from the Page Lines company, www.pagelines.com. I have used the Whitehouse Pro theme and the Platform Pro theme to great effect for multiple businesses. Look at the examples on their site or take a look at one of the businesses I helped found, www.clienttypes.com. Both of these themes have a lot of configuration options that may be a little overwhelming but I still find it infinitely better than building a site from scratch. Furthermore, both of these themes look professional "out of the box."

Other competitors I have not tried personally but have recommendations about from other experts I work with include Thesis Framework from http://diythemes.com/ and Builder from http://ithemes.com/. Take a look at the options and decide which is best for you.

Web Fluent: The Faster, Easier Way to Build Your Web Business

iBlogPro4   WhiteHousePro3   EcoPro   StationPro3

From what I have seen of the three companies, the Pagelines themes are more configurable, the Thesis theme is more of a complete solution (many common business functions already included), and the Builder theme is the most basic. There are many more themes available, just pick the one you like.

2. Hosting

You are typically going to be looking for a host that can inexpensively provide great support and "up time." If you have not yet purchased a URL, many hosting companies will happily take care of both the domain registration and hosting.

To make it easy, choose a host that has easy automatic installation of WordPress. This really takes a lot of the "developer" work out of building your own website.

I have used www.Godaddy.com on many occasions with great success and ease. They will handle the domain and hosting very cheaply and install WordPress for free with a couple of clicks. Godaddy is one of the best, fast, inexpensive and easy options for a company and for a direct link use the below: ttp://www.godaddy.com/hosting/wordpress-hosting.aspx

As for me personally ... I have graduated to the big leagues of hosting and use www.Rackspace.com. I am able to manage dozens of sites with incredible support and reliability. A much bigger price tag, but worth it in the right circumstances.

3. Basic Setup

My goal when setting up a website is to have the basic structure and architecture in place quickly. I have taken the approach over many years that it is better to have something up and running than to wait for the perfect website. This allows me to having a functioning professional website almost immediately and I can then add all the fancy bells and whistles I really want as I start working through the later steps. This way if a snag occurs on one of the more advanced features that takes a while to work out you still have a functioning website up and running.

Web Fluent: The Faster, Easier Way to Build Your Web Business

There are a lot of great resources out there on "getting started with WordPress." Youtube and your favorite search engine will give you dozens of tutorials. The WordPress.org site also has lots of great material. After creating my account and logging in the first thing I do is upload my theme. WordPress does all the work, just go to the Appearance > Themes section and choose upload. Then I create the basic business pages—Home, Contact Us, About Us, Blog (common in business now), Product (or Service or whatever fits your business), FAQs or Testimonials and other relevant pages.

Next I run through the Settings section; key things I do here to improve the professional look include:
- General:
    - Fill in the all the basic info (I frequently turn off "anyone can register")
    - Reading key trick: Change the "Front Page display" to "A static page"
    - Front page set to the new Home you created above
    - Posts page set to the Blog page you created above

- Discussion: I almost always turn off "Allow people to post comments on new articles," turn on the "Users must be registered and logged in to comment" and the "Administrator must always approve the comment." (This prevents unwanted, unprofessional comments from showing up on your site or blog.)

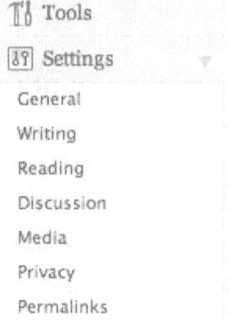

- Privacy: For a business site you really should select "I would like my site to be visible..." Most of the premium themes give you some options to configure fancy home page features like a sliding images, banners and boxes. Also most allow you to configure color options (and other selections from the theme) that fit your business.

WhiteHouse Options *framework*

Here are some screenshots of the options for WhiteHouse. *(Note: There are more options than are shown in the screenshots.)*

Header/Nav *Pages/Posts* *Feature* *On Page*

On Post

Text

Color Options

4. Basic Content

Web Fluent: The Faster, Easier Way to Build Your Web Business

For the most part this step is just inputting your text and images. As I noted before, the goal is still to have a functioning professional website up quickly.

This is the time to get the core business content up—text and images. Steal from yourself, from any brochures, marketing copy, business plans and anything where you have already done the hard work. Again this is a good place to use the broadly available WordPress tutorials for a little help if you get lost.

The great news about WordPress is that when editing a Page or Post there is a visual editor that gives you most of the basic options with a simple toolbar—even an option to upload images or files from your computer right into the Page or Post.

That little feature is one of the big reasons WordPress is so effective for business owners. You can go right in and update the website content yourself quickly and easily.
No developer needed.

5. Plugins and Widgets

Many of the core business "features" you want on your website can quickly and easily be added using pre-built Plugins and Widgets for your website sidebars.

This section is one of the other reasons WordPress is so perfect for entrepreneurs and owners. Assuming WordPress—and your theme—doesn't give you everything you want you can go to the Plugins section, choose Add New > Search, take a look for what you need select Install Now. If it doesn't work the way you want it, you can deactivate it later.

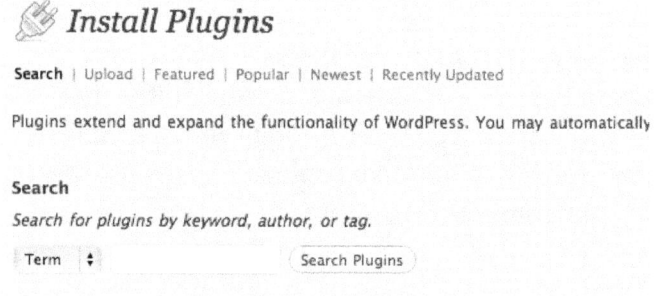

Looking for the best way to find the really good plugins? Use your favorite search engine and put in "wordpress plugin" followed by whatever function you need . If you are using other business-related online software you'll find that many of them provide WordPress plugins for free.

Here are my top favorites in several categories:

Web Fluent: The Faster, Easier Way to Build Your Web Business

- Contact Forms: cforms
- Image Gallery: NextGEN Gallery
- Search Engine Optimization tools: All In One SEO

6. Advanced Setup

This is the phase where you start going back through your website and enhancing it. Here you can add the features that allow the website to drive your business.

Examples of features you can add include:
- PayPal links
- Fancy home page visuals
- Advanced Theme customization (a good theme will help you do a lot of the work to make your site look unique and professional at the same time)

- Pop ups
- Squeeze pages (a signup or sales page with no options to go elsewhere on your site)
- Subscriptions and Signups
- Opt ins
- Membership Site and security
- Google Analytics integration
- CRM (Customer Relationship Management) integration

The best part is that all these extras can be done with existing free plugins. Some do require a little configuration and may require you to try several different options before it works the way you prefer. See the next point for a key tip.

7. Advanced Content

Here is where you start adding the depth that builds credibility to the site. A lot of this is adding sub-pages below your existing core pages or adding videos and other custom media to add dimension and make it easy for your customers/clients to understand and buy your products or services.

Examples of advanced content include:
- All of your terms—Privacy Policy, Terms of Use, etc.
- Integrating youtube video (depending on your needs, the "unlisted" YouTube option is great for this)
- More depth information on your product, background and company
- High quality images, graphs and charts

Web Fluent: The Faster, Easier Way to Build Your Web Business

- Search Engine Optimization efforts
- Additional blog posts/news stories/articles
- Sidebars that drive business and action

Many of the plugins, widgets and themes might need to be put in html instead of having a visual editor. WordPress to the rescue. One of the best things about the WordPress visual editor is that there is a tab to change it to show you the html.

Non-Developer Tip: Create a draft post in WordPress, use the visual editor to design whatever advanced content you are working on for a plugin, theme or widget. When you are satisfied with how it looks, click on the HTML tab and you can just copy and paste that html into the specific plugin, theme or widget. No developer needed.

8. Other Alternatives to WordPress
WordPress is not the only alternative for easy and professional website building. Several others that many experts highly recommend include:
- www.Shopify.com especially designed for e-commerce

- www.Hubspot.com especially designed for marketing and SEO
- www.Weebly.com especially designed for ease of use and non-developers

The primary difference between these and WordPress is that they are typically more restrictive in the options you have available. With WordPress you can always have a developer come in later to add any feature you need.

Another important thing to consider is if you need to have your own credit card processor in the future or if you are happy using Paypal, Google, Yahoo or other processing services. That really goes beyond the scope of this guide.

9. Conclusion

WordPress is a great blend of simple steps to creating professional websites while still providing the business long term flexibility. Most business owners find the ability to modify their own site without a developer a key benefit in moving their business forward. With the
broad support available, ongoing open source development and variety of free additions, WordPress is one of the best options for many businesses.

> ❖ If you'd like Sterling to mentor you and build your new website venture, just send him an email at

Web Fluent: The Faster, Easier Way to Build Your Web Business

quote@bestwebsite.com for a custom quote. Full website design and launch packages start at $1,500.

Making Videos That Bring in Buyers.

Three years ago I shot my first business video using a cheap Webcam that sits atop my computer. The first take was about 8 and a half minutes. I ended up liking it and uploading it to YouTube. It's titled "Internet Marketing - $100,000 in 30-days With Your Website."

In the video I describe how to sell spin-offs of your current Website for a lot of money to other countries around the world because the search algorithms are so specific you need separate websites to reach them.

What this means is, if you have a reasonably successful website in the United States, you can pick-up hundreds of thousands of dollars very quickly just by running a classified ad on a place like BizBuySell to sell duplicates of your website to others looking to buy a proven business model. Then just copy the code to a new Web server and domain name and change the name of the business to something else other than the original name.

The video isn't that great, but the information is. At this point if you type "internet Marketing" into YouTube, it's the second video that comes up for organic results and has been viewed more than 30,000 times. It's currently getting more than 100 views a day which is a big deal because it's really tough to get people to sit through an 8 and a half minute video and it doesn't register as a "view" if they don't watch the whole thing.

So what has been the effect of this creating and uploading this one video? I receive sign-ups every day both for my YouTube

Web Fluent: The Faster, Easier Way to Build Your Web Business

channel and click through traffic coming from that page to my website from people joining my email blog list. I also routinely receive email questions about it and requests for consulting noting the person had watched the video. I'm also sure I get a boost in book sales, but I'm not able to accurately track that.

Having a video that is viewed 100 times a day is as good as holding a conference every day where I'm speaking to 1,000 people because only 10% of them will likely be interested in what I have to say. Since the 100 views-a-day are people who have chosen to sit through the entire video, I can reasonably assume they are interested and engaged with what I'm saying.

My advice. Pick a topic you'd like to talk about that's related to your business. Grab someone with an iPhone, because you can shoot, edit, compress and upload everything right from the phone and get a video out in no time. It might not be great, but at least you are moving in the right direction. And in my case, maybe it wasn't a great video, but it still had a great impact on my business.

Web Fluent: The Faster, Easier Way to Build Your Web Business

Web Trends – Telling the Future and Other Magic Tricks You Should Know About.

I asked Lana Bates, who is a brilliant fore-teller of future trends; to pick a few and give her insights.

So without further ado, here is her latest take on where things are going and how to earn money from it.

By Lana Bates Dir. of Marketing BestWebsite, LLC

ALERT! KNOW THE TRENDS AND BUILD YOUR BUSINESS. IGNORE THEM AND IT WILL BREAK YOU!

I admit I'm a data freak! Anytime there's something new going on I want to know about it. I have bulging file folders and stacks of 3 x 5 cards referencing cool resources and websites, to say nothing about my computer folders and Rolodex.

Just in case there's a few of you out there like me, I'm going to give you a smattering of Technology Trends, Social Media Moves and of course, down-home news about some good ole Search Engine Shenanigans.

But before I do, may I remind you that others have crashed and burned because they failed to see what was coming. Can you imagine how embarrassing to have been the employee in the late 1800s at the United States Patent Office who said we may as well close since everything has already been invented.

Or, how about the heartbreak watching the powerful train corporations languish because they thought they were in the train business and not the transportation business which could have taken them into the billion-dollar airline world of the 20th century.

Sometimes I feel overwhelmed by how fast everything is changing. Maybe you do too. But it's worth it to keep your ear to the ground and your eyes on the real goal—to build a lucrative business that gives you freedom in your life and time to spend with your family and the opportunity to contribute to the world in some small way.

We owe it to ourselves and to those whose lives we touch, to give them the best of who we are. Knowing what's coming will help you do that.

Web Fluent: The Faster, Easier Way to Build Your Web Business

Okay, enough of that! Let's get on with it.

TRAFFIC TRENDS: In the world of internet marketing Traffic Is King! Yes, there's the product, the website, the payment processor, etc., but they all lead up to one thing—making money. And ladies and gentlemen, the only way to do that is to get traffic. If you think most traffic comes from Google you would be wrong. It's said that only 6% of all traffic comes from Google.

And here's the trend—Yes, Google is still a player, but many Internet marketers are tired of the snubs and slaps that Google metes out. Traffic is coming from more and more diverse sources.

Here are the ones to watch: Facebook is becoming more and more powerful. Thousands of marketers are testing Facebook ads. And there is a return to old-fashioned media buying—you know, banner ads and display ads—which has been the darling of traditional marketers forever. Just like investing your money, don't put all your traffic eggs in one basket. Pick one method and learn it well. Then pick another one until you have an arsenal of traffic methods that can make money for your business.

TRENDY SOCIAL MEDIA: Even though Facebook, Twitter and YouTube are sources of traffic, they are still, well ... social. Many people would like them to stay social, but business is getting quite a stronghold. And nowhere is that more true than in the job market or in getting new clients.

One great quote that illustrates this came from the author of **The You Plan** in an interview I saw on TV. "Social media is the New First Impression."

Another quote that shows the pervasiveness of these sites in our lives is— "A social network is now our social proof." In other words, we no longer have to supply lots of testimonials. People wanting to do business with us simply put our name into the search engines and peer into our personal and professional lives based on the social networks to which we belong. Watch for this to become even more important, and be careful what you say.

An excellent resource for staying current on all things "social media" is **SocialMediaExplorer.com**.

MEDIA TRENDS: Streaming video in real time like USTREAM is here to stay. Yes I know, it spits and sputters and stalls but it will get better. Soon we will be putting more streaming video on our own websites with greater confidence.

Two distinct categories of videos are emerging—the homegrown type that we love so well, with the

Web Fluent: The Faster, Easier Way to Build Your Web Business

refrigerator in the background and a barking dog that only we seem to hear but the talking head does not. The second category is the more professional video—shot with greater finesse, detailed graphics and pricey sounding music. Tools are emerging almost every month to more easily make your videos look like the movies we grew up with. (OK, so it's not like the movies but at least maybe like a TV show.) Which category are you? Will the second category take over? Remember, keep your ear to the ground!

Do you have a Google TV? No? Why not? Well all right then, you must not be an early adopter because if you were you would have one already or maybe even two. Sony sells them. I was intrigued and found an article on the web with this headline from **TheChromeSource.com**. "WHY GOOGLE TV MAKES MY CURRENT TV REALLY BORING." If you're like me, you think so much of regular TV really is quite boring, but before you run out and buy one, you should know that Apple is also wanting to throw a hat into the ring with its iTV. Which will win out? Both have pros and cons, of course, but the gamer world will have a big say-so as to who wins out.

MOBILE MASTERY: The world of mobile devices has exploded. (Notice I did not say mobile phones—that term doesn't fit anymore.)

And just like doing business in social media we now can do business with our mobile devices. With a little square gizmo, we can slide a customer's credit card using our own phone. Just like that, we have their money.

And QR codes? Don't even go there! That's another longer story. With those little squares, dots and dashes that are showing up on movie posters, store windows and flyers ... QR codes let us take a picture with our mobile phones to get coupons, go to websites or see movie trailers.

But for a while, the biggest trend will be text campaigns. And it's not just for restaurants with discounts or a business wanting to announce a grand opening. Internet marketers can text their members in ways similar to the early days of email before spam filters made things more difficult. It's going to be open season for a while until eventually it will be regulated just like email.

Get busy on this now by converting your websites to mobile formats and learning how to do text campaigns for a whole new audience. To learn about everything mobile you want to hook up with a major guru who has his mojo together—Dan Hollings. He's the internet marketing guy behind The Secret, one of

Web Fluent: The Faster, Easier Way to Build Your Web Business

the world's most viral movies ever produced—to the tune of $300,000,000. His comprehensive course is at **MobileSuccessFormula.com.**

Want More? Check Amazon for Lanas' new Kindle Single on Web Trends.

Case Study: Great Web Traffic.

Jim Weber 28, formally with ESPN the Magazine, was one of the people who just completed the Mentor Program with me. His website LostLettermen.com is an interesting Case Study for how to get great web traffic.

During the six-week program we implemented a marketing strategy that brought in so many visitors, his site is now the #1 College Sports Alumni Website. I wanted to share how he's done it with you.

Google Analytics:
His Google Analytics shows he currently receives 98,050 Unique Visitors viewing some 392,433 pages on his site every month. And those numbers are

Web Fluent: The Faster, Easier Way to Build Your Web Business

growing. What is most impressive to me is the wide diversity in where that traffic is coming from, as well as how he's been able to generate the traffic in the first place.

Site Usage			
〰	98,050 Visits	〰	4.08% Bounce Rate
〰	392,433 Pageviews	〰	00:01:34 Avg. Time on Site
〰	4.00 Pages/Visit	〰	79.66% % New Visits

He received organic traffic (free) from more than 2,580 different, highly targeted keywords from Google, Yahoo, Bing, etc. Part of the reason the search engines love him so much is because he writes compelling articles every month and submits them to some of the big sports websites like *Sports Illustrated*, *Rivals* and ESPN.

For example, last month Jim wrote an article titled Gatorade Players of the Year and How They Turned Out. He submitted it to the big sites by emailing the article to them; *Sports Illustrated* actually picked it up and linked to it. He received more then 61,907 Views on this page alone last month.

This is at the heart of Web Marketing. Gain the trust and links from the big sites and not only do you get the traffic from them, but the search engines love you because they now trust you.

How Jim Weber Makes Money:
Jim is now making money by offering advertising on his site. He just signed a deal for $2CPM (meaning they pay him $2.00 for each 1,000 Ads he displays) through a bulk Ad provider. But he can make $10CPM if he sells his own. He's just begun to do this using his own Media Kit.

So the math looks like this: At 392,433 Page Views a month and 2 Ads per page, 784,866 Ad displays at $2 per 1,000 Ads views equals $1,569/mo. Once he's selling his own advertising at $10CPM, that is $7,848/mo and if he displays 4 Ads per page, that is $15,697/mo.

Focusing on high-quality articles is much better than quantity. Maybe sports writing isn't your thing, but I'm sure something else is. When I do this for my own site, I think about the most compelling article I could write and who I could submit it to that is most likely to pick it up.

Notes: LostLettermen.com was started in March 2009 and built on a customized *WordPress* template. The database runs the site and is written in standard PHP coding.

Web Fluent: The Faster, Easier Way to Build Your Web Business

Jim Weber – Founder LostLetterman

When Things Aren't Working.

So you've got a Website, Blog, Videos, FaceBook and Twitter account. You've also done Search Engine Optimization, Pay-Per-Click and even prayed once that something would work.

But it's not ... now what?

The best advice I have for this situation, that more than 98% of Web entrepreneurs fall into, is this:

Focus on one thing ... and make it BRILLIANT!

When you look around at those who are successful, you see they have all the things listed above. But what you might not realize is that they almost all started with one thing first, built it slowly, gradually, sometimes painfully ... and everything else expanded naturally from there.

If you're struggling it's probably because you're trying to do too much. Focus all your energies on the one thing you love doing the most, and that will also make you money.

Web Fluent: The Faster, Easier Way to Build Your Web Business

You don't need all these things listed above to start, they are just amplifiers for something you have already made successful.

The Self-Publishing Revolution is Upon us.

For the first time in three years, my first book *Best Website* has earned more money through Kindle sales than printed sales. This is amazing to me and not something to ignore.

For the first time in history, you don't need to ask anyone to publish your book and reach around the world. You can convert your Microsoft Word file into a Kindle Digital Text file for free and have direct access to the biggest bookstore anywhere, Amazon.

If you sell a $9.99 Kindle book, as the author you keep $6.99. You don't even need a full book to start, you can upload a short article called a Kindle Single and sell it at $2.99 and keep $2.10. It's a brilliant way to get your feet wet in the digital publishing world.

And the very first day you start to receive royalty checks and realize you don't need to talk to any customers or deliver and ship anything yourself, might be the first day you get hooked on authorship as a career.

Share your genuine message and it will spread.

My First Book.

Best Website: *Simple Steps to Successful Websites* (2008)
Amazon Paperback Bestseller for two-years and hit #1 on Kindle Web Marketing category.

Best Website shows how to make at least $10,000 to $20,000 a month with your website business.

It shows step-by-step **Domain Name** registration, **Web Hosting** setup, step-by-step **Microsoft Expression Web** web-design examples, **Federal Trademark** Registration and includes a chapter titled *How to Earn $100,000 From Something You Already Have.*

It's surprisingly relevant today; I thought it would be out-dated by now.

Entrepreneur Motto.

I leave you with this.. an Entrepreneur Motto that has taken me ten years to refine.

I designed it and then had it printed on a Sticker using *Moo.com* and then stuck one to the outside of my business Journal that I use to write down my ideas.

I read it every time I open my Journal to make sure I'm in the right frame of mind.

Tear this page out and
put it someplace you'll notice.

Web Fluent: The Faster, Easier Way to Build Your Web Business

This is a promotion piece mounted on foam, and then hung from the back of my beach chair. The photo almost looks fake, but it's un-retouched. (Printed/mounted by Mpix. Photo by me.)

Gratitude..

A big thank you to my Mom(**Lana**) and Dad(**Ted**) for letting me hash out many, many ideas with them and provide their valuable insight and wisdom. Without them I'd be lost.

Also to my older brother **Sterling** for providing a brilliant WordPress article. He's incredibly gifted at taking a big complex subject and distilling it into useful information.

And to my little brother **Morgan**, whose kind words and encouragement helped me through some of the times my ideas weren't working.

Also, to **Nancy Perez**, the social media maven who let me bounce a number of ideas off her and provide sage advice in return. You're awesome! ..and so are your Meetups.

To Marc Baldwin and his fantastic professional proofreading business **Edit911** who not only edited my first book, but this one as well.. and definitely made it MUCH better. I highly recommend his services at **Edit911.com**

Web Fluent: The Faster, Easier Way to Build Your Web Business

Also, thank you to **99Designs** who did a fantastic job at organizing the Book Cover design contest for me; they gave me 49 different designs to choose from for this book, many of them unbelievably brilliant. (Check my blog for a link to see the other entries.)

A warm thank you to full-of-positive-energy Social Media Marketer **Shama Hyder Kabani** who let me show her early drafts of some of my more daring posts and provided wise and astute advice in return.

And to **Les Kandel**, who at 74 years young has been getting-after-it the last four years building his parenting site, **BaBearz.com** into an excellent portal for parents to learn anything and everything about early childhood. A great resource indeed!

My Amazing Dad.

Right near the completion of writing this book, my Dad—Ted Bates, was interviewed by Jim Axelrod of **CBS Evening News** in the home I grew up in, in Wichita KS. He was the only employee out of more than 2,000 to be interviewed.

It was for a piece that ran January 18th 2012 titled **"Jilted by Boeing, Wichita Workers Feel Duped."**

My Father has worked as a *Systems Engineer* at Boeing for 34 years. Most of the time it's when things get "messy" —is when he is called in to fix them.

Boeing chose to close its Wichita plant; even though it promised it thousands of jobs if they won the Tanker program. Which they did.

Web Fluent: The Faster, Easier Way to Build Your Web Business

My Dad was asked what he thought of Boeing's decision—his response was elegant, intelligent and empathetic.

I sure do admire him.. every day!

Thanks Dad.

Notes: http://www.cbsnews.com/8301-18563_162-57361398/jilted-by-boeing-wichita-workers-feel-duped/?tag=mncol;lst;10

Web Fluent: The Faster, Easier Way to Build Your Web Business

Nelson Bates, 36, is a #1 bestselling business author, 16-year Web entrepreneur and founder of some of the Internet's most popular websites.

In 1995 Nelson pioneered the web marketing industry with the original **Internet Marketing Center**™ website. In 2000 he was snapped-up as the lead web master for **Walt Disney World®**. In 2002 he launched his own web design company, **Blue Aspen Web Design**™ (successfully sold) that he built into the Web's largest design company with 86 independent operators.

In 2003 he invented the Web's most-used Website Appraisal™ system to value internet companies and built **BuySellWebsite**® LLC (successfully sold) into the world's largest marketplace to buy and sell Web businesses.

In 2007 he started his current company **BestWebsite**® LLC that teaches others how to build successful Web businesses of their own.

His book ***Best Website**: Simple Steps to Successful Websites (2008)* has been an Amazon paperback best-seller for three-years running and even hit #1 on Kindle for Web Marketing.

Nelson is known for giving useful, simple advice about how to start, build and promote successful Web businesses.

main site: BestWebsite.com
blog: NelsonBates.com

As always, those on my blog email list heard these ideas first, I'd be honored if you'd join me: Sign up at NelsonBates.com

Web Fluent: The Faster, Easier Way to Build Your Web Business

The Password is: smile

Please share this book with a friend.

They'll thank you.

www.ingramcontent.com/pod-product-compliance
Lightning Source LLC
Chambersburg PA
CBHW051218170526
45166CB00005B/1946